Nine Peaks

Nine Peaks

Poems in Classical Chinese

Rhee Sukho

A Dual-Language Edition
With Parallel Texts

Translated by
Sung-Il Lee

RESOURCE *Publications* · Eugene, Oregon

NINE PEAKS
Poems in Classical Chinese

Copyright © 2024 Sung-Il Lee. All rights reserved. Except for brief quotations in critical publications or reviews, no part of this book may be reproduced in any manner without prior written permission from the publisher. Write: Permissions, Wipf and Stock Publishers, 199 W. 8th Ave., Suite 3, Eugene, OR 97401.

Resource Publications
An Imprint of Wipf and Stock Publishers
199 W. 8th Ave., Suite 3
Eugene, OR 97401

www.wipfandstock.com

PAPERBACK ISBN: 979-8-3852-2268-1
HARDCOVER ISBN: 979-8-3852-2269-8
EBOOK ISBN: 979-8-3852-2270-4

Cover Art: Part of "山水圖" ("A Landscape") by Yi Sang-bŏm (李象範 1897–1972); The whole landscape (47.4 x 133.4cm) was drawn by brush in ink in 1948. Courtesy of the Museum of Yonsei University

In Homage to

Professor Rhee Sukho

訪隱者

隱士茅屋何處尋
漠漠雲裏柏松深
紅花交葉舞而笑
黃鳥隔枝踊又吟
出世立身治國揭
入山求道潛心沈
夕嵐長嘯老益壯
弄月詠風便鍊金

九峯 李錫浩

Holograph manuscript of *Visiting the Man in Retreat* (p. 16)

Contents

Preface   11

Poems

Bitter Rain   15
   苦雨   15
Visiting the Man in Retreat   16
   訪隱者   16
The New Moon (I)   17
   新月 (一)   17
The New Moon (II)   18
   新月 (二)   18
Watching the Flood   19
   觀漲   19
Cool Air Blowing Anew   20
   新涼   20
Exultant over the Sky Clearing Up   21
   喜晴   21
Visiting a Man Living in Retreat   22
   尋隱者   23
The Shade of Trees   24
   綠陰   25
Ascending Mount Do-bong   26
   登道峰山   26
Newborn Swallows   27
   新燕   27
In Praise of My Own Self   28
   九峰李錫浩自讚   28
Upon My Friend Colonel Roh Being Discharged   29
   祝演柏盧載寬大領轉役   29
Congratulating Professor Kim Tae-sŏng on Earning a Doctorate   30
   祝金泰星教授取得文博   30
At the Grave of Tan-jong the Boy King   31
   參拜莊陵   31

Upon Visiting the Grave of Prince Ŭi-an 32
    宜安大君墓奉審有感 32
Upon Turning to Seventy 33
    七十自歎 33
Composed on My Seventy-seventh Birthday 34
    喜壽自歎 35
Upon Turning to Eighty 36
    八十有感 36
Upon Reaching the Age of Eighty-eight 37
    米壽自歎 37
Upon Turning to Ninety 38
    九十自述 38
Remembering My Elementary School Teacher 39
    安恩卿老師贊 39
Grieving over the Death of My Friend Rhee Chang-hak 40
    謹弔李昌學兄 41
Recollecting My Life 42
    我歷行 43

About the Translator 63

Preface

Throughout the long history of Korean literature the mainstream of poetic composition was in classical Chinese, although composing poems in the vernacular continued to flourish all along, thanks to the invention and promulgation of *han-gŭl*, the uniquely Korean orthography invented and put to use in the mid-fifteenth century. Nowadays, however, only a limited number of people trained in classical Chinese are still engaged in composing poems in it. The poet, whose works are translated into English for inclusion in this book, is a scholar who has devoted all his life to studying classical Chinese literature.

Professor Rhee Sukho (李錫浩), pen-named Gu-bong (九峰, 'Nine Peaks'), was born in 1932 at Yong-in County, Kyŏng-gi Province, Korea. He studied classical Chinese literature at Seoul National University, earning his baccalaureate in 1958 and his doctorate in 1970. He taught at his *alma mater* as an instructor while carrying on his post-baccalaureate studies. He was appointed a professor of Yonsei University in 1973, and taught there till he retired in 1997. He has written several books on classical Chinese literature, including studies on the philosophy of Kong-zi (孔子) and of Zhuang-zi (莊子), as well as translations of and interpretative essays on classical Chinese poetry. A distinguished scholar of classical Chinese literature, he also published a collection of his own poems composed in classical Chinese, entitled '九峯漢詩集' (*Poems of Gu-bong in Classical Chinese*) in 2018.

A senior professor in the College of Liberal Arts of Yonsei University, Dr. Rhee Sukho is a man I have ever wished to take after, although his field of study is far from mine. He is a reticent man; but when he utters a word without showing any sign of his feelings, he makes the listeners smile at his sense of humor and at the piquancy of the hidden meaning of an apparently innocuous comment. He doesn't wish to impress others with his erudition, or to reveal his inner life to the outside world. Probably this explains why many of the poems included in his book, *Poems of Gu-bong in Classical Chinese*, from which I have chosen the pieces for translation, are eulogies on his acquaintances, not about his own self. It may be an indirect way of telling his readers what he really wishes to tell. I have translated only the poems that explicitly express his personal feelings on certain occasions, ending the book with a long poem of his autobiographical account.

The autobiographical account at the end of this volume uninhibitedly tells how the poet led a poverty-stricken life in his youthful days, while trying to attain his life's goal. The poet is not abashed to recount the poverty-stricken life of his youthful days. Though the readers have no obligation to read through all the detailed account of the hardship and misery that the poet has gone through in his life, it can be read as everyman's life story, while the poet unabashedly tells his own. For his life-story he relates can be a universal one.

I dedicate this slim volume to Professor Rhee Sukho, who has led a life devoted to scholarship, while enduring all the hardship and the onslaught of sad occasions in life.

Sung-Il Lee
February, 2024

Poems

Bitter Rain

As I lie down to take a nap on an early summer day,
Sudden wind blows to darken the sky and block sunrays.
A gush of rainfall may make my whole body refreshed;
But this dreary downpour over ten days only wearies me.
When will all the dampness disappear, clean and clear,   5
To let bright sunrays fall on every nook and corner?
As I, awakened from my dream, cast my eyes on the world,
I hear only moan and groan over the drought and hunger.

(Composed on May 15, 1968)

苦雨

初夏午睡臥草堂
忽然黑風蔽日光
聚雨一過身爽快
長霖旬降心煩狂
何時天下無濕陰   5
到處地上有乾陽
夢覺遍看宇宙間
旱魃怨聲及八荒

Visiting the Man in Retreat

Where can I find the hut of the man living in retreat?
Deep in the clouds, only pines and birches stand thick.
Commingling their petals, red flowers dance and smile,
While orioles sing, frolicking on the crossing branches.
Having extolled his name in helping to rule the land,   5
He entered the mountain to let his soul attain tranquility.
Though grown old, he sings loud and long in the evening fog;
Befriending wind and the moon, he digs into life's mystery.

(Composed on June 5, 1968)

訪隱者

隱士茅屋何處尋
漠然雲裏栢松深
紅花交葉舞而笑
黃鳥隔枝蹈又吟
出世立身治國揚   5
入山求道潛心沈
夕嵐長嘯老益壯
弄月詠風傾鍊金

The New Moon (I)

Xī Shī, a woman of heavenly beauty, died for her country, Wŏl.[1]
When she died, her two eyebrows flew away to settle in the sky:
One, hung aloft in the blue sky, sobs in grief inconsolable,
The other, afloat in the boundless ocean, looks down silently.
The two eyebrows far off from each other long to be together;   5
But, once separated, they have no hope to be adjoined again.
When will it be that the crows build a bridge across the sky?[2]
Then her brows might meet again, as she frowns behind a veil.[3]

(Composed on July 18, 1968)

新月 (一)

西施爲越死
身沒峨眉飛
一掛碧空咽
一浮滄海睎
相連意馬願   5
各別幽期違
烏鵲何時得
再成嚬繡幃

---

[1] Xī Shī (西施), a woman born in Wŏl (越), one of the ancient kingdoms in China, is known to be one of the legendary beauties, who incurred the downfall of the monarchs or generals, who fell in love with them.
[2] Folklore often has the allusion of the birds flocking in the sky to make themselves stepping stones for any two separated to have reunion.
[3] The legend tells that the moments of the supreme beauty of Xi Shī were when she frowned, tightening her eyebrows.

The New Moon (II)

As the moon looms between the clouds,
Silence and tranquility reign all around.
If there is a beautiful woman, who will
Reveal half of her face over the mountain,
Even a man incorrigibly enslaved to gold   5
May become one with a heart most tender.
The way the moon cast her beam on River Chae-sŏk,[1]
Even now she moves me to compose, as Li Po did.

(Composed on July 18, 1968)

新月 (二)

玉蟾出雲間
四郊寂寞時
若有一美人
隔山露半眉
不惑守錢奴   5
唯賞多情兒
昔照釆石江
今遺李白詩

---

[1] The legend tells that Li Po (李白) stepped into River Chae-sŏk to grab the moon reflected on the stream, thus drowning himself, but ascending to the sky to become immortalized.

Watching the Flood

When will the rain stop pouring down as if the sky leaks?
The dreary rainfall continuing day after day lowers my spirit.
Houses are immersed in water to have only the roofs left seen;
The fields are inundated, while cultivated paddies crumble.
Though children yell in joy over plentiful catches in the nets,   5
Peasants weep in grief over all the harvest fallen to ruin.
The season of drought is hardly over when flood sweeps;
Why is it that the Creator's whim is so hard to predict?

(Composed on July 22, 1968)

觀漲

漏天豪雨何時停
連日長霖心鬱結
住宅浸流屋頂浮
郊原汎濫田畦滅
投網兒輩豐魚呼   5
失稼農夫凶歲咽
旱魃纔經又水災
造翁戲劇何其譎

Cool Air Blowing Anew

Cool air blows again from the suburban field,
And the chill is renewed in the cold moonbeam.
Crickets start being seen only to hide out again;
Glowworms start glimmering only to fade away.
Beneath the bridge over a stream plump fishes jump;   5
And rice-flowers spread their scent far over the field.
All the works the heat of summer has made put off
Henceforth ask for being taken care of in much hurry.

(Composed on August 26, 1968)

新凉

新凉入郊墟
蕭新冷月光
蟋蟀生已變
螢火影欲藏
川梁肥魚躍   5
原野稻花香
因炎滯百事
從此日漸忙

Exultant over the Sky Clearing Up

As I look up on the sky after the rainy spell is over,
I see no speck of cloud in the crystal-clear expanse.
The far-off mountain looms at the edge of the sky,
And the long river flows on, dividing the wide plain.
In the paddies the farmers' straw-hats are seen, while   5
On the narrow lanes the colorful skirts flutter in the wind.
Gazing on the scenery, I gradually forget my presence,
And emerge from the oppression of the living world.

(Composed on July 27, 1968)

喜晴

霖後望穹窿
清淨無點雲
遠山天際見
長江平野分
田中出黃冠   5
路上翻羅裙
凝視漸忘我
蕭灑脫塵氛

Visiting a Man Living in Retreat

On this holiday, where shall I go to spend the time?
Upon arriving at Nam-han Fortress, I park my car.
As I stroll, enjoying the scenery of the deep-seated vale,
A small cabin looms, hidden in the wood of the heights.
Upon my inquiry about the owner of the humble dwelling,   5
A man with a ruddy face and white hair comes out slowly.
With tender eyes cast on an intruder from the dusty world,
He admits me into his hut with full smile on his face.
To an unknown visitor he tells his thoughts uninhibitedly,
For, living alone, he has read the books reserved for the hermits.   10
Staying away from the dusty world, he remains stout and strong;
Having been away from the buoyant world, he is free from greed.
In front of his hut, butterflies flutter over his yard for vegetables;
From the beehives above the steps, honey flows on plenteously.
In the thick shade of the exuberant trees daylight lasts only too short;   15
And in the haze surrounding the mountain earthquake roars.
Standing awhile on this spot of the earth, I forget the dusty world;
My very body seems to have turned into the trunk of a tree.
Having remained ignorant of what the man in retreat knows,
I suddenly come to realize what I should've known far ahead.   20

(Composed on June 12, 1968)

尋隱者

休日消風何處去
南漢山城急停車
深山幽谷翫賞步
峻嶺林中一茅廬
借問此屋誰何主 　　　　　　　　5
紅顏白髮出門徐
凝視不關俗人輩
欣然微笑迎仙居
對坐肯論鍊金術
獨居精讀神仙書 　　　　　　　　10
身壯脫俗仙骨肥
心遠浮世物慾虛
門前菜田蝴蝶飛
階上蜂巢蜜蜂餘
繞樹綠陰午日短 　　　　　　　　15
圍山嵐氣地籟噓
久立此界忘娑婆
吾身變爲一寒樗
由慾不知隱者情
到此忽覺心地初 　　　　　　　　20

The Shade of Trees

How soon and fast do the sprouts in early spring bloom and grow
To turn into tall trees along the roads to block the heat of the sun!
The green growing thick fills our eyes, pleasing them with its shade;
And the absorbent shade is cast on the earth to render it dark,
Inducing a pedestrian traveler to take off his wear and wipe off sweat,   5
As an old man listening to his talk falls dozing, weary of the jargon.
Through the folded leaves, the orioles send out ear-pleasing notes;
And the cicadas on the tree branches vie to chirp and sing out loud.
When summer heat is at its height, trees grow exuberant and thick;
So the frost-bit leaves in the autumn wind will look even lovelier.   10
When the newly dyed leaves color all the mountains soaring up,
And the biting wind blows ferocious, fallen leaves will fill the vales.
Then the woodcutters will sumptuously cut off the woody harvest;
Put in the furnace to burn, they will surely turn into heat and smoke.
Burnt in a flame, something turns into ashes to warm others—   15
The way to make vegetables grow, things are thrown into furrows.
So, men must take after the virtue of the green shade of the trees,
And attain the ultra-merit of self-sacrifice for everlasting glory.

(Composed on July 15, 1968)

綠陰

新春嫩葉何暇長
路邊高樹蔽炎天
青青萬綠觸目爽
隱隱陰影撫地玄
披衣過客休斂汗
聽談老翁坐自眠
隔葉黃鸝送好音
抱枝鳴蟬爭調絃
夏季三伏草木盛
無情金風霜葉妍
新鮮丹楓染萬山
朔風吹落溝壑填
樵童不惜採取去
入竈點火變熱煙
焚身燬他化灰爐
培養蔬菜棄陌阡
人間須效綠陰德
殺身成仁功名全

Ascending Mount Do-bong

Escorting our mentor, we ascend Mount Do-bong to see
The peak soar so high and the water flow so crystal-clear.
When the Creator made the world, He paid special attention,
So the extraordinary-looking rocks might soar high to the sky.
The highest peak resembles the gong hung in the main temple;   5
The green water-flow may be meant for leading to Nirvana.
Looking down from the top, we feel like climbing even higher;
As we lie down drunk at the foot of the mount, rainbows loom.
As we bid farewell, promising a better climbing for next time,
Evening wind blows to wash away what lingers in our hearts.   10

(Composed on August 1, 1968)

登道峰山

陪師攜友登道峰
山高水麗都神功
造翁開闢特留意
奇巖怪石聳天空
主峰恰似梵鐘懸   5
碧溪疑是極樂通
山頂瞰來時願登
山底醉臥見彩虹
今番忽然留餘約
夕陽歸情洗心風   10

Newborn Swallows

A pair of swallows flew in late in the spring, and built a nest on the crossbeam;
Soon afterwards I heard the newborn chicks' chirping coming from the nest.
At the outset, it was hard to tell them from the chicks of other birds;
As they grow, they begin to resemble their mother, or others of their breed.
As days pass, they get more and more used to taking the feed in their mouths,　5
And, fluttering their wings, improve their skill of flying day after day.
For humans, youth is the time that can be esteemed to be life's zenith;
For birds and animals, their babyhood is the time when they are loveliest.
Peck and drink as much as you can, so that you may grow fastest;
Get ready for your upcoming journey to the south before cold wave comes.　10

(Composed on August 29, 1968)

新燕

暮春樑上來作巢
忽見新雛發歡聲
遽爾難分他種鳥
及長漸肖其母兄
開嘴仰食日益慣　　　　　　　　　5
翩翼數飛隨時更
人生青春極華美
禽獸稚小特麗精
多啄多飲速成長
寒前一齊江南行　　　　　　　　　10

In Praise of My Own Self

Born at the foot of Mount of Nine Peaks as a boy of pigmy size,
I belong to the clan that takes pride in descending from a royal family.
Early in my life I ploughed the land, but left my home later on,
Though late, to pursue new learning, and settled in the royal town.
I've trod the road leading to the world neither of brush nor of sword,   5
Only to become a wanderer, who has attained neither wisdom nor fame.
From now on, I'll give up all I've aspired after, and enter a mountain—
Who knows? I may then arrive at the hillock where peach-blossoms bloom.[1]

(Composed on May 8, 1978)

九峰李錫浩自讚

九峰山下生微身
本貫我朝王裔孫
早習農桑離故鄉
晚聞新學到天閣
非文非武邯鄲步   5
無智無名楚客魂
此後盡遺入深嶽
終當必覓桃花源

---

[1] '武陵桃源,' literally meaning "the plain where the peach-blossoms bloom," that is, the imagined place where only happiness and eternal joy pervade.

Upon My Friend Colonel Roh Being Discharged

Born enwrapped by the spirit of the mounts guarding your ancestral village,
You have been a man of filial piety, patriotic zeal, and neighborly love.
For how many decades have you risked your life to extol your soldierly honor?
How many springs have gone, each time you thought it could be the last?
You were born to have an insight into what would be the best way of living;   5
And now at your age of full maturity, you've finally become a peaceful citizen.
I pray you enjoy the rest of your life filled with magnitude and benevolence,
And may comfort and happiness be your lot in recompense for your career.

(Composed on August 30, 1979)

祝演栢盧載寬大領轉役

駕山精氣凝全身
大孝大忠又體仁
揚武懸命數十載
死生存沒幾回春
先天英智計前途   5
不惑卓才爲逸民
厚德善行振世界
富貴福祿比無倫

Congratulating Professor Kim Tae-sŏng[1] on Earning a Doctorate

A boy standing on the bridge of Dae-dong River in Pyŏng-yang
Was swept by a crowd of refugees, and finally found himself in Seoul.
Wherever he turned, there was none, whose face he could recognize;
Wherever he wandered in, there was none, who was happy for reunion.
Working for living at daytime, and reading in the lamplight till dawn broke,   5
He swore to heaven and earth that he would attain his life's goal.
On this day, when a doctoral degree bestowed on him is gratifying,
Pain digs deep into his heart, for words of gratitude to his parents are blocked.

(Composed on August 25, 1979)

祝金泰星敎授取得文博

浿江橋上一孩嬰
混入難民纔到京
環視四方無面識
周行天地非歡迎
腐心切齒勉耕讀   5
誓海盟山期晚成
今日文星尤燦爛
但哀不報兩親情

---

[1] Professor Kim Tae-sŏng (金泰星, 1933~2023) studied English literature at Yonsei University, and later taught there till he retired in 1998. As a teenager he alone left his home in North Korea to be away from the brutal rule of the communist government, and managed to graduate from Yonsei University, despite the penury he had to endure alone in the war-torn country. While teaching at Yonsei, he shared friendship with Professor Rhee Sukho, who was one year older than he.

At the Grave of Tan-jong the Boy King[1]

Where is the grave of the boy king put to death by his usurping uncle?
It is where pines and birches grow thick in a remote county, Yŏng-wŏl.
There you'll see a small mound on a hill, where sunlight showers on
To be shadowed much too often by the clouds that billow, darkening over.
Emperor Sŏng became a magnificent ruler, thanks to his guardian uncle;[2]   5
But the last king of Chok became a bird weeping nightly, blood-choked.[3]
This young monarch, whose life was taken at a flowery age of seventeen,
Makes a haphazard passerby shed tears rolling down to wet his sleeves.

(Composed on November 22, 1979)

參拜莊陵

莊陵遺蹟於何尋
寧越僻村松栢森
突兀岡南一掬墳
斜傾域內數雲陰
成王業績治民本   5
望帝寃魂蜀鳥心
十七芳年不意逝
後人哀慕淚沾襟

---

[1] King Tan-jong (端宗, 1441~1457), grandson of King Se-jong the Great, was the 6th monarch of Chosŏn Dynasty. Prince Su-yang, his uncle, usurped the crown, and eventually killed the boy king, his nephew, whom he put in exile at a remote mountainous place called Yŏng-wŏl.
[2] King Sŏng (成王) of Chu (周) of ancient China ascended the throne as a boy. But under the guardianship of his uncle he became an excellent ruler of the kingdom.
[3] The last monarch of the ancient Chinese kingdom Chok (蜀), after the downfall of his kingdom, became a bird weeping blood-choked every night, as the legend tells. As a matter of fact, King Tan-jong composed a heart-wrenching poem alluding to the nightly weeping of the bird, which reflects the heart-breaking agony he himself underwent.

Upon Visiting the Grave of Prince Ŭi-an[1]

I've been feeling guilty over not having paid a visit to your grave;
Now I've come here, I feel relieved to have my guilt lightened.
Your mother's ambition made you the inheritor of the kingly crown;
The fight among your brothers slashed off your glory of seven years.
What difference would it make, wherever your small body was buried?   5
Far from the royal town, you were buried in this remote, hidden valley.
Looking down on this narrow gorge where narrow winding lanes crawl,
The sun and the moon will be appalled to see what human greed has left.

(Composed on May 21, 2014)

宜安大君墓奉審有感

未曾奉審未消恨
禮畢只今心自平
十歲國本母后慾
七年世子同氣爭
小身埋骨可何所   5
幽谷深山遠離京
九折羊腸險陝路
天上日月眼開驚

---

[1] Yi Sŏng-gyĕ ascended the throne as the first monarch of Chosŏn Dynasty in 1392, after deposing King Gong-yang, the last monarch of Koryŏ Dynasty. His fifth son, Pang-won, who ascended the throne as the third king of the new dynasty, killed his younger brother Pang-sŏk, born by his stepmother, Queen Shin-dŏk, his father's second wife, at the uprising he initiated in an attempt to seize the power. Yi Sŏng-gyĕ had designated Pang-sŏk as the crown prince, despite the fact that he was much younger than his sons given birth by his first wife. When the young crown prince was slaughtered by Pang-won, he was only seventeen years old. He official appellation was 'Prince Ŭi-an.'

Upon Turning to Seventy

In olden days people used to say: "One can rarely stay alive to reach seventy."
But nowadays many people live to pass this wonted limit of growing old.
People in the prime of life cast cold eyes on those who've turned into old age;
Youngsters pass by them, rapidly carrying their steps, caring not who tarries.
But within an aging one's heart and body, hot blood still flows on;   5
And his muscles and sinews are strong enough to withstand life's hardship.
Whither fled are the four old men, who secured safety at their times of turmoil?
In the mountain where they sojourned remain only the handles of their axes.

(Composed on August 25, 2001)

七十自歎

昔人稱古稀
今溢老翁婆
青壯白眼視
兒童急步過
心身流熱血   5
筋力耐風波
四皓去何處
商山留斧柯

Composed on My Seventy-seventh Birthday

"Reaching seventy of age has been rare since antiquity."
So did Tu-fu write in a poem entitled "The Winding River."
In olden days, being seventy years old meant longevity; but now,
Being seventy years old is equivalent to being sixty in olden days.
Passing the age of seventy, I've grown seven more years older; 5
So the rest of my life will be a journey that will fade into dusk.
Leading a life in solitude after sending my wife away ahead,
I now worry about my son's future darkened by loss of occupation.
It is not a false saying that, once misfortune comes, another follows;
It is also true that ill luck approaches, when good prospect is seen. 10
I hum the lines Tao-chin composed, worrying about his son;
And I read the lines on chasing off poverty, over and again.
Heaven must have seen some merit in me, for I was given birth;
Then why is it that I find myself always suffering in ill luck?
I'd rather believe I am fated to suffer more and more as I grow older; 15
Rising up after falling time and again ought to be the way I must opt.

(Composed on July 3, 2008)

喜壽自歎

人生七十古來稀
子美曲江詩一句
以前古稀意長命
今世七十比初度
古稀過後又喜壽　　　　　　　　　5
將來餘生黃昏暮
阿婦先亡獨鰥居
豚兒失職尤危懼
禍不單行不虛言
好事多魔非謬誤　　　　　　　　　10
數吟淵明責子詩
頻讀揚雄逐貧賦
天必有用出我生
如何這樣每不遇
老益試鍊本八字　　　　　　　　　15
七顛八起我行路

Upon Turning to Eighty

Sunlight has flowed, as a white foal flees through a gap in the fence;
And I find myself a man who has lived for well over eighty autumns.
My oldest son is struggling to overcome the aftermath of a stroke;
And my second son leads a precarious life, clinging to his occupation.
People say, "Life is a sea of pain"; and it is not a saying vainly uttered.   5
The only way to be free from life's pain is to surrender oneself to nature.
Having lived alone for over five years after sending my wife away,
I still suffer from all the onslaught of pain and worries that cling to me.

(Composed on August 4, 2011)

八十有感

白駒過隙日光流
荏苒至今八十秋
長子中風勉治療
次兒任職企長留
人生苦海非虛語   5
無為自然乃解憂
妻死獨居五歲餘
險難連續不勝愁

Upon Reaching the Age of Eighty-eight

The slow flow of time is like that of a watery stream,
And I've already lived for eighty and eight more years.
My feverish passion has all been exhausted and gone,
And only decrepitude has rapidly seized me in its grasp.
Having donated ten thousand books to the village library,   5
I am now free from the worries over the unread books.
In all affairs of life, beginning and ending repeat themselves;
Serving the public good with good will is the way for rebirth.

(Composed on September 23, 2019)

米壽自歎

苒苒歲月如流水
我齒此年米壽年
過去熱情盡破散
現今老妄急蕃延
萬卷書籍贈鄉里   5
千曲愁心轉熟眠
每事輪廻又始作
奉公積善再生緣

Upon Turning to Ninety

Having passed my eighties, I've now turned into ninety.
Callous years fleet by, not caring those they sweep over.
My beloved wife, who has joined the spirits in the other world,
Beckons me in my nightly dream, and urges me to join her soon.   5
All phenomena remain the same; what changes is my reception.
Living alone, I do not care about my beard growing too long.
"As you have been waiting for me so far, wait a little bit more.
When I finish all the work yet to be done, I shall join you soon."

(Composed on July 3, 2021)

九十自述

八十已過今九十
無情歲月過隙速
棄我賢妻入仙界
待我促來送夢信
萬象如前人心變   5
獨居生活長蓬髮
百忍之情少期待
世事早畢即承順

Remembering My Elementary School Teacher

When I was a child attending an elementary school,
I was a kid whose head was full of feelings and doubts.
But she imbedded the knowledge clearly in my small head,
So that I might step into the world of learning I should enter.
Her boundless love was wider than the expanse of the sea;
And her heart was brimful to overflow the bound of the pond.
If a person is devoted to his or her ardor, it'll be recompensed:
For the fame of a teacher will remain and be extolled forever.

(Composed on April 18, 1997)

安恩卿老師贊
小學幼年期
多感多惑時
明瞭傳學識
緻密啓良知
慈愛溢滄海
恩情滿碧池
積功必有績
萬世令名師

Grieving over the Death of My Friend Rhee Chang-hak

My friend Chang-hak, who passed away just today, has been
Dear to me, with his surname Rhee, though of different descent.
In our childhood we went to the same village school;
In our boyhood we attended the same elementary school.
During the war, he was drafted to fight in the Northern army   5
And belong to the troops that invaded the South of our country.
Then he had to be put in Kŏ-jĕ Island as a prisoner of war.
Released from the camp, he joined our army to fight the North.
Having reached River Yalu that marks the border of our land,
He had to retreat, pushed down by the swarming Red China's army.   10
He barely survived the rain of the bullets showering like hell,
And having been discharged, returned home to plow the land.
All the untold stories of the war and its pain he had gone through
He promised to tell people in every particular before his death.
Before he could keep his promise, he met the end of his life's term. 15
Who can now count all the jewels that his telling could've spilt?

(Composed on February 7, 2018)

謹弔李昌學兄

今日召天昌學兄
咸安李氏恒多情
幼時同里書堂友
少年國校同窓縈
事變強徵義勇軍　　　　5
編成南侵人民兵
被虜收容巨濟島
釋放轉入國防行
北進統一到國境
人海戰術踏回程　　　　10
謀免戰死彈雨裏
除隊歸家務農耕
萬難克服體驗談
約束口述盡吐聲
躊躇未發身先去　　　　15
其實貝何時細評

Recollecting My Life

I was born in a village called Mok-sin Li,
In Won-sam District of Yong-in County,
At a hut crouching in a secluded nook,
To a poor peasant's family residing there.
Since the cot was a crumbling hovel,   5
Fingers got frozen, ready to fall out;
And the dried-up field barely farmable
One could reach only after crossing hills.
The paddies numbered no more than thirteen,
Of which the small one was no bigger than a foot.   10
Even those did not belong to my parents,
But were a rich family's they were allowed to plow.
Even before the harvest was done halfway,
Every year the landlord threatened forfeiture of the land.
When the landlord's delegates came at harvest time,   15
My parents served them cooked chicken and dry seafood.
When they had finished their meal and left our home,
We rushed to the table to grab and devour the leftover.
When I turned into the age to attend a kindergarten,
My father made a wooden rack for carrying things on back,   20
And, giving it to me, told me to help with the chores at home.
So my life as a young laborer at home had its beginning:
Following my father, I carried compost and manure, and
Helped my mother to draw and carry water for use at home.
    When I turned into eight years of age, I entered a *sŏdang*.   25
That private school was at the foot of Mount of Nine Peaks.
The old teacher who taught the children was Master O Midang,
Who had the fame as a nonpareil man of learning.
When he taught us *Dong-mong-sŏn-sŭp*, the primer for children,
He explained to us even the hidden meaning between the lines.   30
Having had my eyes open to the joy of reading and learning,
I could tell that my knowledge was growing as days passed.
My mentor's praise encouraged me to work harder and harder,
To let me excel in repeating what we learned in previous lessons.

我歷行

我鄉龍仁郡
遠三木新里
後洞僻村家
農夫生草鄙
頹落一間屋 5
嚴冬寒墮指
乾畓四斗落
遠隔越幾峙
畓數十三塊
狹小如足趾 10
其地非我物
借耕富豪主
秋收半打作
每年與奪土
脫穀舍音來 15
殺鷄又市脯
食後退床上
殘饌爭手拊
幼年兒戲期
父作支架子 20
給我曰勞作
自此協農始
從父負堆肥
隨母汲泉水
八歲入書塾 25
九峰山下在
老師吳微堂
博學冠當代
敎我童蒙習
行間細敎誨 30
我始覺學問
日就月將態
師讚我尤勉
背講獨無挹

My mentor's third son, on the other hand, so it happened,   35
Became a rebel, or a lawless resolute, as he grew older.
While my mentor's praise encouraged me to work harder,
He scolded his son all the more for not working as hard as I did.
His son's anger grew bigger and bigger as the days passed,
And he went to the extreme, letting his fury burst out.   40
One day he forced me to sit on a swing tied to a tree;
He climbed the tree and defecated on me sitting on the swing.
With my whole body stained with the filth he dropped on me,
I screamed and wept in irrepressible anger and humility.
Though my pals in my class felt sorry to see me in distress,   45
They could not help laughing and clapping their hands loudly.
After that incident, I stopped going to the *sŏdang*,
And stayed at home, not letting my gift of learning known.
    When I turned to ten, I entered an elementary school,
And I had to walk more than ten *li* to arrive at the school.   50
During summer I dragged a pair of wooden clogs,
And in winter I plodded, wearing a pair of straw-mats.
When I came back home, I spent time on cutting grass;
On holidays, I cut the tree branches to burn for heating.
One day, in the setting sun, I was leading a calf held by a strap,   55
Bearing a load of grass and branches collected on its back.
Its feet got caught in a string of entangled grass,
And, having fallen down, it ran away in the grip of fear.
I held hard onto the leading rein with my two hands;
And it made the calf run away ever faster on the slope.
The calf, stricken with fear, kept running on the slope.   60
Exhausted, I fell into a stupor, with my judgment all gone;
Then crescent moon was up above, shining on the world.
    Two years before the country became liberated,
My family moved to the nook called Sŭng-juk Valley,
Just with the hope of escaping from the life of poverty.   65
It was located over the hill, about three *li* away;
But our family had secured there a modest piece of paddy,
Not to mention nine hundred *p'yŏng* of gravel-filled land.
My whole family, only for the sake of our survival,

師傅第三男　　　　　　　　　35
長成無賴輩
師賞我進就
深責他愚昧
每日他積憤
暴發盡行悖　　　　　　　　　40
命我鞦韆戲
登樹放糞尿
我身被污物
痛哭哀絶叫
衆友竊憐我　　　　　　　　　45
環視拍掌笑
以後我退塾
在家藏才調
十歲入小學
通學十里過　　　　　　　　　50
夏日引木屐
冬天着草靴
歸家剪牧草
空日伐樹柯
夕陽負草來　　　　　　　　　55
以手牛靷拖
足蹴堅結草
顚覆牛犢蹉
雙手固執紖
驚牛疾走坡　　　　　　　　　60
氣盡心昏憊
初月照娑婆
解放二年前
欲免耆且生
移徙勝竹谷　　　　　　　　　65
越嶺三里程
中畓十斗落
礫田九百坪
全家糊口策

Remained busy day and night, plowing the small piece of land. 70
Upon the country's liberation, thanks to the land re-allocation,
Our small piece of land came into our family's possession.
As our family's income became double of what was before,
Poverty could be relieved, to make our life much more bearable.
   After graduating from the elementary school, I could not 75
Find any way to make my schooling go on any further.
While spending day after day on plowing a piece of land,
I could not find a speck of pleasure, not the smallest one.
Then an old man surnamed Han in the neighborhood of ours
Told my mother that she'd better send me to a school; 80
Having had my parents' approval of furthering my schooling,
I felt a gush of courage and zeal shooting up in my heart.
At that time, in the town of Yong-in, a new school named
Tae-sŏng Middle School happened to be built and inaugurated.
The distance between the school and my home was almost fifty *li*; 85
But eating and sleeping away from home was unthinkable.
So, my father went to an aunt of mine living near the school,
And, having persuaded her, managed to solve the problem
By offering to send to her three *mal* of barley in the summer,
And three *mal* of rice in the winter, to pay for my upkeep! 90
   While studying hard during the three years' attendance,
I also did not neglect building good friendship with my pals;
And several friends of mine helped in a variety of ways,
And I could finish that interim schooling of mine successfully.
Since there was no high school in the town of Tae-sŏng, and 95
Each was about to take his own way, all becoming separated,
Our school created a new class for learning practical skills.
I decided to stay on before looking for a job for livelihood.
So, while prolonging my stay there for one more year,
I kept on studying, befriending the dim lamp every night. 100
   However, barely a few days after I started my schooling,
That cursed war broke out, tearing up the whole country.
Now the whole country had become a bloody battlefield,
I could not but give up my schooling, despite my ardor for it.
While I was hiding at home, away from the blood-shedding, 105

晝夜力籽耕
光復土革後
償還爲自營
所出倍於前
貧苦少減輕
小學畢業後
進學無道理
每日務農事
秋毫無欣喜
隣居韓老人
教我勸先妣
終當父母許
意慾再震起
當時龍仁邑
新設泰成中
相距半百里
宿食亦困窮
父訪堂姑母
哀切吐深衷
夏麥冬白米
三斗宿費充
勉學三年間
交友又積功
諸朋協各面
及期乃有終
泰成無高校
他地各分散
新設職業班
解決求職難
我留一年間
螢火對雪案
入學數日後
六二五動亂
全國變戰場
學業亦中斷
歸家蟄居中

70

75

80

85

90

95

100

105

The whole country turned into a hell called "People's Republic."
Though the Red Army urged me to join 'the glorious war,'
I did not beat the drum, but hid in the nook not to be found.
   After the capital was retrieved on September twenty-eighth,
The war-front started moving northward, as the war continued.   110
But as the Red China's army swept down like a sea of humans,
Our government had to give up our capital city to retreat again.
So, after the humiliating retreat on the fourth of January, 1951,
All had to move to the extreme edge of the land in the south.
   Limping like a cripple, I managed to arrive at Tae-gu.   115
Unable to solve the grave issue of being fed and accommodated,
I joined the army for defense of the land away from the war-front
To serve as an officer fulfilling missions of a non-combatant.
While our army and our opponent alternated victory and retreat,
The war finally fell into limbo on the thirty-eighth parallel line.   120
Now that the army for defense below the warfront was dismissed,
I could return home and finally be with my long-missed parents.
My parents were more than delighted to see me returning home,
And I and my brothers hugged one another in overflowing joy.
Having had a long time of separation with no news exchanged,   125
We spent a sleepless night, telling how we had fared till then.
   In a neighboring village called Chŏng-nyong, it happened,
A unit of the national armed forces kept its base for staying.
The soldiers from it robbed cows and raped young women;
The villagers could not stand their outrageous acts of crime.   130
Whenever we heard about their disgraceful acts of crime,
The villagers shuddered at their beastly and shameful acts.
We happened to have a calf we were growing at our home;
It was a cute little creature with a docile temperament.
Fearing the soldiers might take it away by force from us,   135
My father smeared ashes and oil on the skin of the calf.
One day soldiers came to our home, and wished to pull
The calf away, though we vehemently protested against it.
Our father told them the calf was infected with disease;
Then they pored on it, and no more insisted on its forfeiture.   140
Since then, after the soldiers left our home empty-handed,

急變人民國
赤軍勸入隊
不應深屏息
收復九二八
勝勢急進北 110
中共人海戰
再次移社稷
一四後退時
避亂向南極
跛行到大邱 115
不可解宿食
入隊防衛軍
擔當後方戰
兩軍進退間
小康三七線 120
解散民防軍
歸鄉纔反面
父母欣迎我
兄弟撫相見
其間無消息 125
共坐徹夜傳
隣村青龍里
國軍支隊留
奪牛犯處女
悖惡不勝憂 130
人聞此消息
含怨以爲譬
吾家一牛犢
體小性溫柔
父想被奪時 135
牛皮塗灰油
一日軍人來
欲牽我小牛
父曰牛得病
凝視無要求 140
其人退去後

We didn't have to worry about having the calf taken away.
    After a short rest, my wish to return to school revived,
And my dream of it would return, shooting up like a mirage.
Then the rumor floated around that an elder cousin of mine   145
Was staying at Chŏng-ju, a town people thought relatively safe.
So I decided to move to Chŏng-ju myself and seek him out
And find out whether I could stay at his place for a while.
For at that time Chŏng-ju High School had added a class,
And was ready to admit more students than it could before.   150
So I could enroll in the high school as a second-year student,
For which privilege my father had to sell the calf for tuition.
My friends, who still remain dear to me now I've grown old,
Were those who befriended me in those days now far ago.
    However, barely after the lapse of one year's schooling,   155
Financial pressure forced me to discontinue my attendance.
I had to leave Chŏng-ju to return home crestfallen, only to
Make my parents feel sad over my discontinuing schooling.
My friends, having heard the news, made an arrangement
For me—so I might get transferred to another school.   160
So I managed to enroll at Su-wŏn High School this time;
My academic record was also transferred together with me.
Barely after three months since I started studying there,
I managed to fill up the number of years for graduation.
During the three years when I enrolled in the high schools,   165
The actual time spent on studying was barely over a year.
Sleeping here, eating there, without any settled place,
I could not achieve much, though my will was ever firm.
At my first attempt at a college entrance examination
I failed to make it, earning the disgrace of being a flunky.   170
Upset by my failure, I chastised myself to start anew,
And, laboring in daytime and reading at night, I persisted.
Next year, I took the college entrance examination again,
And was admitted to the department of my second choice,
The Department of Chinese Language and Literature;   175
But I tried to widen the range of my study well beyond it.
I solved the problem of room and board by teaching kids,

乃無慮牛愁
少憩欲進學
空想蜃氣樓
風聞遠戚兄 145
避亂在淸州
下淸搜所聞
相逢暫時留
其時淸州高
增班募學優 150
編入二學年
賣牛納束脩
當時廣交友
今日好朋儔
不過一年後 155
窮勢迫身邊
去淸急歸鄕
兩親心不便
親友聞消息
轉學急斡旋 160
編入水原高
學籍亦重遷
受業三個月
艱辛卒業年
高校三年間 165
學業一年餘
東宿西家食
意强實力虛
最初大入試
落榜不名譽 170
憤起再出發
畫耕夜讀書
翌年再應試
合格二志望
專攻中文學 175
廣閭積敎養
敎兒寄宿食

And by taking odd jobs I managed to be free from penury.
Having worked for four years while carrying on my studies,
I felt my eyes had become clearer and my heart bigger. 180
   That year I married a woman. Thanks to my fortune,
She happened to be a woman of warm heart and grace.
She urged me to carry on with my studies, and,
Encouraged by her, I entered the school for graduate work.
Every morning my wife headed to her school to teach, 185
And I myself did not neglect my own studies to carry on.
The daily routine repeated itself without any deviation,
And time fleeted by like lightning in the flick of an eye.
   When our first child was born in our rented room,
We became a family with one more for it to accommodate. 190
So with the help of a loan we bought a small house,
A house we claimed to be ours for the first time in our life.
Two bedrooms and a wooden floor lying between them—
Our baby had enough space where he could totter around!
Two years later, another child was born, this time a girl— 195
My wife led two kids, a boy on his feet, a girl on her back.
In order for her to raise her children as best as she could,
She stopped working awhile to concentrate on family life.
Then, when a military coup broke out all of a sudden,
I was dismissed from my occupation, that of a teacher. 200
   My mother, who had been staying at our old home,
Had never been free from physical frailty she was born with.
Only the year before, she had suffered the attack of a stroke;
Henceforth, she had never remained healthy and strong.
One day, my younger brother came to see me urgently; 205
I instinctively could tell that things were not going well.
Although our son was suffering from measles,
We all rushed to my old home where my mother was ailing.
Stricken by a stroke, my mother was lying in her room,
With half of her body paralyzed and immobilized. 210
After taking care of my mother's illness for six months,
My father came to lose his wife to lead a lonesome life.
My own son, ailing with measles, was waved from

雜役免窮狀
四年遂畢業
開眼心曠放   180
其年我婚姻
內子眞淑媛
妻勸我學問
進學大學院
每日妻出勤   185
我亦學不倦
日程正反覆
歲月如馳電
長男出呱聲
貰房增一口   190
借錢買小家
平生初所有
兩房一小廳
吾兒隨意走
二年又生女   195
携子負女婦
內子勉育兒
休職執箕箒
忽發五一六
我亦解印綬   200
在鄉我慈母
本是弱體質
昔年有痼疾
平素無寧日
一日弟急來   205
直感事不吉
長男紅疫中
歸鄉急驅率
慈母腦卒中
身痲臥內室   210
看病六個月
父親喪配匹
長男紅疫癒

Receiving treatment, and lost his ability to hear and talk.
What *karma* do I carry on in this present life of mine,   215
And suffer all this pain, with no joy following after?
Lamenting thus, not knowing whereto I should turn,
I wandered to wherever medicine men of fame were.
Carrying my child on my back, I visited many a hospital,
And shedding tears, I besought the doctors to cure him.   220
When I found out that no doctor was able to cure him,
My heart got torn to pieces, unable to endure the pain.
Since then, we endured all the difficulties of raising him.
Telling of it would be beyond the reach of my tongue.

    Time fleeted by, as a flowing stream does,   225
And the next year our second son came to be born.
A brick house, though covered with a slate roof, was
Not spacious enough to take in a couple and three kids.
To upgrade my status, I devoted myself to learning,
And put the burden of livelihood on my wife's shoulders.   230
Carrying all the burden as a school teacher and a mother,
She struggled to do the work both at school and at home.
But fate is not to be resisted against or complained about;
I never heard a single word my wife uttered in complaint.

    As I wished to lead a career as a university teacher,   235
I taught at several universities, not caring where they were.
"Do all you can, and wait for Heaven's verdict," they say:
When suffering has lasted long, pleasure is bound to come.
Having taught as a part-time instructor at many a college,
I finally found my permanent home at Yonsei University.   240

    Of the three major pleasures that life can yield to us,
The joy of teaching students is the supreme one.
Having started my career of teaching in the year 1959,
I retired this year at the age of sixty-five, as any others.
I started at the middle school annexed to a teacher's college;   245
Then I moved to Bo-sŏng High School to teach older kids.
Then I taught at more than a dozen universities and colleges.
Wherever I went, my concern was to teach what I'd learned.
Having settled at Yonsei University as my final destination,

終當爲聾啞
前生我罪何　　　　　　　215
多難好事寡
長歎不措處
名醫尋都野
負兒到病院
呼訴淚如瀉　　　　　　　220
諸醫終不治
抑寃不能下
其後養其兒
艱難不可寫
歲月如流水　　　　　　　225
後年生次男
瓦葺斗屋裏
夫婦子女三
立身我勉學
生計妻負擔　　　　　　　230
敎童又育兒
萬苦耐不堪
命運不可逆
毫無不平談
我欲留大學　　　　　　　235
講義走北南
盡事待天命
盡苦則來甘
講師十二年
延世作搖籃　　　　　　　240
人生三樂中
敎育最優先
己亥立敎壇
今年方停年
併中始訓導　　　　　　　245
普成執敎鞭
大學十餘校
到處勉師傳
延世終着地

I've done my best to fulfill my task as a teacher and a scholar.　　　　250
While teaching my students and learning from teaching,
I have fulfilled the mission I assigned to myself in youth.
Wearing hair turning white, carrying around a body old and ailing,
I have returned to the green pasture, leading my family.
When I was in the prime of my life, in my youthful days,　　　　　　255
The grand aspiration I harbored was comparable to others'.
The friendship I shared with others was genuine and pure;
I ever respected my teachers and remained loyal to them.
In expanding my knowledge, I have ever valued its depth;
Engaged in learning, I've ever aspired to reach its zenith.　　　　　260
　　Man tends to think highly of his predecessors in learning,
But is apt to take lightly what his juniors are capable of,
For, not knowing what his students may be able to attain,
He more feels like praising and admiring his predecessors.
Even if a mulberry field would turn into a sea in time,　　　　　　265
The ancient sages' teachings are to be retained by all means.
Kim Sŏng-tan, a scholar who lived in the early Ch'ing dynasty,
Wrote a vehement defense of the ancient sages' writings,
And intending to leave instructive words for posterity,
He left it as legacy for those who would live in later ages.　　　　270
I, thanks to the wisdom and virtues of the ancient sages,
Have been blessed, breathing the fragrance of old writings.
Life is ephemeral, and fleets away in the blinking of an eye;
And we all must end up lying in lonesome grave mounds.
If I am not allowed to leave a poem, though a poor one,　　　　　275
What can I give to you, my students, as my gift for you?
The six books Kim Sŏng-tan praised in his writings
Will forever last, as long as they are read and studied.
　　I am a man of poor endowment and meager learning;
So composing lines may be beyond what I can accomplish.　　　　280
Having now retired from doing my work as a teacher,
I'll return with my wife to the village where I was born,
And living in a small cottage with a thatched roof,
Remain happy in the room warmed by burning wood.
Growing vegetables in the yard adjoining my cottage,　　　　　　285

心身竭力全
教學相長中　　　　　　　250
已盡青雲緣
半白體老病
率家歸園田
我亦盛年時　　　　　　　255
雄志人比肩
衷心交學友
恒時思師賢
知識博而精
學問務窮研　　　　　　　260
人思先輩深
關心後進淺
不知後生畏
只頌先賢善
桑田變碧海　　　　　　　265
專守奮訓典
清初金聖歎
痛哭古人辯
寄與後來人
留贈後人文　　　　　　　270
我被先賢德
滿喫文香薰
人生存剎那
從當歸孤墳
不留此拙詩　　　　　　　275
何物贈諸君
聖嘆六才子
萬世永傳聞
我本無才學
作此尚過分　　　　　　　280
今日停年後
與妻歸故鄉
草家三間裏
火木溫突房
耘籽菜麻田　　　　　　　285

I shall wait for my friends to come to chat on a bench,
And paying no attention to what goes on in the world,
I shall not care whether the seasons shift fast or slow.
Keeping Tao-chin's writings on a shelf for books,
Having sheets of white blank paper spread on a table, 290
I shall spend half of a day doing chores of light work,
Drawing myself to the desk, whenever I feel like;
When I find some drink at home, I shall wet my throat;
If I feel elated somehow, I shall hum a few lines of verse.
As I shall feel self-sufficient in the midst of the leisure, 295
How could I ever think about going back to the world?

   Since olden days aging up to seventy has been rare;
So pretty soon I shall be considered a man of old age.
Even when I was barely past the middle of my fifties,
I was stricken by stroke, an ailment hard to deal with. 300
Having tried all available ways of treating that ailment,
I could put it in control only after struggling for ten years.
One must control food intake and maintain peace of mind;
But the prerequisite is to restore a good heart condition.
Wholehearted devotion moves Heaven, as they say; 305
Gradually my heart started to regain its regular beat,
And I could move my limbs as freely as I wished to;
But, most of all, I turned into a man of strong willpower.
When Heaven wishes to impart a mission to a man,
Heaven first puts him on a trial and tests his willpower. 310
What did Heaven see in me and think it useful,
Putting me on a trial when I was about to face old age?
Life slips away as a foal steals out through a gap,
And it fleets by like a dream one may take as an age.
Grasshoppers do not know how spring shifts to autumn, 315
And titmice nestle on the same single branch of a tree.
A man's life lasts for the span of a flickering moment;
But one harbors the illusion of being able to live for eternity.
A rear-horse, counting on its self-deluding 'immense power,'
Ignorant as it is, confidently stands against a rolling cart, 320
And, fighting among themselves, raising their horns,

友來登草堂
無關世上事
不問時炎涼
書架淵明書
卓上白紙張 290
半日輕勞動
時時對書牀
有酒飲一杯
乘興弄詞章
此中有自足 295
何再思行藏
七十古來稀
不遠我齒至
知命後半期
得病最難治 300
百方勉治療
十年纔執轡
食補兼心補
于先脫心悸
至誠則感天 305
漸次回心地
運身能自由
思考尚強記
天將降大任
先苦其心志 310
我有何用材
老來再驗試
人生駒過隙
盧生夢一炊
蟪蛄無春秋 315
鷦鷯巢一枝
人生存瞬間
渴望永劫期
螳螂信自力
拒轍不知危 320
蝸角之相爭

Snails desperately try to decide which one is the winner.
　Having realized how I did go wrong in the past,
From now on, I shall do my best to become benevolent.
I shall dedicate myself to upbringing the younger ones,　　　　　325
And whole-heartedly help them in encountering all affairs.
Now the leaves changing their color emanate reddish hue,
Making all the mountains soar high in their utmost beauty.
While the twilight throws its last beams on the fading hill,
The setting sun sinks into the pond where it will immerse.　　　　330

(Composed on April 13, 1997)

必決死雄雌
我覺昔年非
今後專德施
獻身爲後生　　　　　　　　　　　325
萬事勉驅馳
楓葉吐紅炎
萬山極妍姿
落照烘霽中
夕陽入咸池　　　　　　　　　　　330

About the Translator

Sung-Il Lee was born in 1943 in Seoul, Korea. He studied at Yonsei University, University of California at Davis, and Texas Tech University. He taught English literature at Yonsei University from 1981 till he retired in 2009. Presently he is Professor Emeritus of Yonsei University.

He has published thirteen volumes of Korean poetry in English translation, including *The Moonlit Pond: Korean Classical Poems in Chinese,* listed as an Outstanding Academic Book of 1998 selected by *Choice*. He received the Grand Prize in translation in The Korean Literary Awards of 1990, and the 4th biennial Korean Literature Translation Award in 1999, given by The Korean Culture and Arts Foundation.

www.ingramcontent.com/pod-product-compliance
Lightning Source LLC
Chambersburg PA
CBHW061249040426
42444CB00010B/2318